The Great Livery Companies

of the

City of London

To Dalma

A glimpse of the new Hall of the Grocers' Company

The

Great Livery Companies

of the City of London

Their Halls Depicted By
DENNIS FLANDERS
ARWS

CHARLES SKILTON
LONDON

Type composition by
The Lancashire Typesetting Co Ltd
Salop Street, Bolton
Printed in Great Britain by
Fletcher & Son Ltd
of Norwich
and published by
CHARLES SKILTON LTD
90 The Broadway
London SW19

CONTENTS

FOREWORD

By Sir Ian Bowater, GBE, DSO, TD, Lord Mayor 1969/70

THE LIVERY COMPANIES of the City of London for the most part had their origin in monastic backgrounds. It was, in fact, the monasteries which introduced not only learning in medieval times but skills and trades. From these origins sprang the craftsmen who for their own protection tended to form themselves into Guilds which in turn trained and educated their apprentices. Rules of conduct for Master and Apprentice alike were laid down in fair but firm principles and measures for protection against unfair trading and sometimes even against foreign competition were introduced.

The centre of a Livery Company's activities was the Hall, the place in which the Master or Prime Warden, assisted by members of the Livery known as the Court of Assistants, presided. It was here that penalties for shoddy work, idleness, or ill behaviour were meted out to the culprits, and those penalties sometimes went to the extent of expulsion from the Craft or Mystery.

Dennis Flanders brings to the notice of those who study his work a lively conception of the beauties of these ancient Halls and their precincts. Not many have survived the erosion of planning and two wars. Once, most Livery Companies possessed their own halls and accompanying administrative offices for the clerks and their staffs. Today only 29 such halls exist, although at least two are being rebuilt. The present-day Livery Companies are the administrators of considerable charitable funds derived from foundations of past Liverymen and from gifts and legacies. These are used in a number of directions and in particular for the maintenance of schools and almshouses and they also provide educational scholarships and support universities and the arts, as well as encouraging in some cases the trades from which they derive their origins. Some, such as the Fishmongers and the Goldsmiths, retain considerable powers within their trades, and at Goldsmiths Hall the Hall Mark on all gold and silver objects is stamped after testing. The Halls, which are generously lent to those not possessing their own, are also the scenes of social occasions and each year are visited by the Lord Mayor. The granting of honorary Freedoms takes place ceremonially at the Hall or in the Binding Parlour and it is always a great and picturesque occasion.

I am sure that this book of Dennis Flanders's delightful and characteristic drawings will be welcomed by all lovers of the City and of the history of its ancient Guilds.

IAN F BOWATER
Alderman and Haberdasher

ARTIST'S NOTE

FIRST AND FOREMOST I wish to record my great debt of gratitude to the late Sir Bruce Ingram, the renowned Editor of the *Illustrated London News*, whose idea it first was that I should make a series of drawings of the Halls of the twelve Great Livery Companies of London. It was a formidable task, and there were moments when I felt unable to draw another chandelier; but he never failed to encourage, and the work was duly completed. In addition, I would like to record my thanks to his nephew, the Deputy Editor at the time, Mr Hugh Ingram, for his help in arranging permission for me to visit the various Halls and for generally smoothing my path.

There are others I wish to thank: the Clerks of all the Companies and their staffs, who assisted me in many ways while working on their premises; Mr Charles Skilton, my publisher, who has spared no pains in the detailed preparation of this book; Mr Roger Hutchings and Mr Andrew Pennycook, who have written the notes that accompany the drawings; the present Directors of the *Illustrated London News* who have extended their permission to reproduce; to Mr Arthur Hall in his capacity as Keeper of Prints and Pictures of the Guildhall Library, who commissioned the picture of the interior of the Guildhall, in which hang the banners of the twelve Great Companies, and to his successor Mr Godfrey Thompson, the present Keeper; and to my good friend Mr James Howgego for allowing us to use the drawing here which neatly ties up the close connection between the Livery Companies and the City Corporation; and finally, I would like to thank Mr John Francis, Liveryman of the Grocers' Company, for commissioning a drawing of the interior of the new Grocers' Hall, just lately risen upon the ashes of the old, burnt down in 1965, and for allowing us to include it in this book.

As for the merits of the Livery Halls themselves, they all have their particular charm. Recalling them all together upon the inward eye, there can be no doubt that the Fishmongers' is the most satisfying of all. It stands by itself at the City end of London Bridge, a rather plain classic building, and its windows look out upon the Thames. Inside, on the first floor, the Banqueting Hall and its attendant reception rooms are heavily decorated with gold leaf and are most magnificent. The sun, as it passes over the southern sky, shines upon the rippling surface of the river, which in turn reflects upon the golden ceilings and cornices, giving a rare and remarkable beauty to these lordly rooms. One might be in a Venetian palace. The drawing room gives particular pleasure. Annigoni's portrait of Her Majesty takes pride of place, and in the mirror opposite is reflected the tower of Southwark Cathedral. What a place to draw!—and who would expect such beauty in the heart of the City?

The Goldsmiths' Hall is, as one would expect from the nature of their work, the most lavish in decoration, and its façade in Foster Lane, with its splendid sculptural trophies is an exciting piece of architectural design, carried out in the baroque manner, not common in London.

Among other splendours that remain in one's recollection is the row of enormous pillars striding round the apsidal end of the Drapers' Hall, a full length royal portrait hung between each; very effective is this. Then there is the recollection of the sweet smell of sandal-wood that delights the senses of whoever opens the door of the Court Room of the Worshipful Company of Skinners. The panelling put up in about 1670 is still giving out its lovely aroma. In the midst of the Merchant Taylors' Hall is a garden, completely secret, for no trace of it appears to the man in the street, and one might speculate on the financial value of such a piece of land in the heart of the Square Mile.

In the Vintners' Hall is a fine display of banners, and rich panelling in the Court Room which has the reputation of being the oldest inhabited room in the City. Then there is the new Grocers' Hall, just completed after the disastrous fire of 1965, with its startling John Piper tapestries and glorious iron screen (this last astonishingly refurbished from the ruins of the old).

The Ironmongers' Hall is unique in being the only one to be built in the period between the Wars, as its predecessor was the only Hall destroyed in the First World War.

Of the Halls that have been rebuilt after 1945 there are three among the great twelve. The Haberdashers' is traditional classic, the Mercers' seems all pillars and mirrors, and the Cloth-workers' is distinguished by a courtyard, entered through decorative iron gates, and inside the Hall, a truly splendid collection of Hanslip Fletcher original drawings of London scenes, of the kind that used to decorate the pages of the *Sunday Times* for many years.

The Salters' have not yet been able to rebuild their Hall. In order to make the collection complete, therefore, I have made a set of drawings from old prints and photographs.

DENNIS FLANDERS

NOTE: Most of the drawings are carried out in ordinary lead pencil, but in a few instances, the medium used is monochrome wash with a touch of pen and ink. Half of the originals are in the possession of the Companies concerned, and the remainder in the Guildhall Library and Art Gallery.

The Guildhall

Denis Flanders

INTRODUCTION

THE LIVERY COMPANIES of the City of London are as diverse in their historical backgrounds as in the surviving documentary evidence of their dates of foundation. The earliest of them evolved from the twelfth and thirteenth century Guilds in which fellow traders or craftsmen associated voluntarily for the mutual protection of their common interests and for benevolent purposes. The earliest Guilds took the names of patron saints and met at churches of their patronal dedication; it is uncertain whether the trade or craft connection preceded the religious purposes of association, but the two functions certainly evolved together.

At least two of the Guilds may have been established in Saxon times: those of the Saddlers and the Weavers. A document ascribed to within a century of the Norman Conquest refers to 'ancient rights' governing the relations of the Saddlers with the monastic Church of St Martin-le-Grand. The Weavers' Guild was at least as venerable: its earliest Charter is believed to have been granted about 1105, and it is recorded as having contributed to the Royal Exchequer only a quarter of a century later.

The formal incorporation of most of the ancient Guilds dates from the Tudor and Stuart periods, but many of them were evidently exercising more or less effective control of their trade or craft within the City (and sometimes beyond its boundaries) before receiving the Royal Sanction. Earlier, the Guilds were licensed, as we know from the list of those fined for meeting illicitly in 1180. The transition from Guild to Livery Company is generally reckoned from the adoption of a livery and in many instances the earliest Royal Charters merely confirmed existing rights dating from 'time immemorial'. Many of the Charters were re-granted in subsequent reigns, often with extended powers. Most of the Companies originally enjoyed some statutory rights of inspection and the correction of abuses within the trade or craft they represented, and in the cases of the Goldsmiths and the Fishmongers certain statutory functions are still exercised to this day. Some Companies—as exemplified by the Apothecaries and the Stationers—traded corporately until the nineteenth century. Others still retain certain corporate privileges, such as that of the Dyers and the Vintners to share with the Crown the ownership of swans on the River Thames. The latter Company also retains the individual privilege of its Freemen to retail wine by the glass in London and certain specified cities, seaports and coach-road towns, without sanction of a justices' licence.

At an early stage in the municipal evolution of the City the Livery Companies acquired civic rights which are still maintained, such as the exclusive enfranchisement of their Liverymen to elect the Lord Mayor and Sheriffs, a system unique in the local government of the United Kingdom.

There are eighty-four surviving Livery Companies, including some—such as the Curriers, the Bowyers, the Fletchers, and the Loriners whose function no longer exists or is now greatly restricted. Others—as for instance the Whitawers, the Fustarers, and the Megusers—have vanished with their extinct trades. Many of the surviving Companies retain only nominal connections with the trades of their designations, but some (and in particular the Goldsmiths, the Salters, the Vintners, the Farriers, and the Spectacle Makers) are still directly involved in the trades they represent, especially as regards technical training facilities. A few have adapted to modern techniques in lieu of obsolete skills: for example, the Pattenmakers are now associated with the manufacture of rubber footwear, the Horners take an active interest in the plastics industry, and the Fanmakers encourage the development of all kinds of mechanical fans.

The term 'livery' refers to the distinctive costume formerly worn by Liverymen of the Companies, and which in mediaeval times distinguished them on ceremonial occasions. These distinctive liveries were richly contrasted in colour and were varied from time to time, as for example that of the Grocers: scarlet and green in 1414, scarlet and black four years later, scarlet and blue in 1428, and crimson and violet in 1450.

The relative precedence of the Companies was formerly the subject of many acrimonious disputes, of which some concluded in violence and bloodshed and penal or capital sentences. The present order of precedence (including the division between the Great and Lesser or Minor Companies) evolved by reason of their intrinsic importance and wealth and hence their order of priority in the processions that marked every civic ceremonial occasion, of which today's Lord Mayor's Show alone survives. The Great Companies struggled fiercely to achieve and to maintain their status, but paid for it bitterly during the Tudor and Stuart Reigns and the Commonwealth when they were subjected to enforced loans of which only a fraction was ever repaid. It is greatly to their credit that despite these setbacks their charitable trusts and educational foundations have remained inviolate and, in most instances, extended and diversified in the light of changing conditions.

Apprentices were formally enrolled and Freemen admitted to citizenship at Guildhall, the centre of the City's municipal administration, the venue of the Court of the Lord Mayor and Aldermen, the principal place of civic assemblies, and the meeting place of Companies lacking their own premises.

There is mention of a Guildhall at least as early as 1135 and it is now certain that the hall stood upon part of its present site by at least the late thirteenth century; but the Great Hall of which elements still survive was erected between 1411 and 1425. Much of it, including all its timber work, was destroyed by the Great Fire of 1666, and restored three years later; and other improvements and extensions were made in 1789, 1865, and 1909. The further severe fire damage of the Second World War—in the bombing raids of December 1940—was restored by 1954, with additional amenities.

The main entrance porch, which still shows some fine fifteenth-century vaulting, leads directly to the Great Hall, of which the present stained glass windows designed by Sir Giles Gilbert Scott record the names and dates of the Mayors and Lord Mayors of London to the present day. The blazons of the Livery Companies are depicted around the cornices, and banners embroidered with the arms of the Twelve Great Companies hang with strikingly decorative effect. There are also imposing monuments to commemorate Admiral Lord Nelson, the first Duke of Wellington, the first Earl of Chatham, and Pitt the Younger. In the minstrels' gallery are the carved figures of Gog and Magog, the legendary giants associated with the City, and with the Guildhall site in particular. Beneath the Hall are two mediaeval crypts: the Eastern Crypt (restored 1960–61) which is contemporaneous with the fifteenth century Hall; and the Western Crypt (restored 1971–73) which is almost certainly part of an earlier thirteenth century Guildhall.

The Mercers' Company

Mercers Hall D'Flanders

THE MERCERS' COMPANY is first among the Great Livery Companies of the City of London in rank and precedence—an honour that was disputed for centuries by the Grocers—and among the most ancient and venerable of them. Its twelfth century origins are traced to a Fraternity of Mercers who associated for 'mutual aid and comfort' during the reign of Henry II, by whom they were almost certainly formally recognized as a corporate body, since they were not recorded among the 'adulterine' guilds fined for meeting without the Royal Licence in 1180.

Among the prominent Mercers of this early period was the first Mayor of London, Henry FitzAlwyn, who served for twenty-four years from 1189. So was Gilbert à Becket (the father of St Thomas of Canterbury), who served King Stephen as Port Reeve of the City, its senior civic office prior to the establishment of the mayoralty. Soon after the Saint's canonization in 1173 the site of his birth, just off Cheapside, was presented by his sister Agnes and her husband, the Baron de Helles, to the Military Order of St Thomas the Martyr and endowed as a hospitaller house and church, with which the Mercers' Company was to become more and more closely connected. From the end of the twelfth century the Order (by then 'of St Thomas of Acon') was preoccupied with crusading service in the Levant, and transferred the responsibility for the London house of its name to the Mayor and Corporation in 1327. The Mercers, who held their meetings there from soon after 1380, eventually received charge of the foundation as its 'defenders and advocates' in 1514; and after its suppression by Henry VIII in 1538 the Company purchased the freehold of its site and buildings four years later. Mercers' Hall and Chapel still occupy the same site today, having been rebuilt in 1682 after the Great Fire and again in 1958 in consequence of destruction by enemy action in 1941.

Mercers were originally retailers of silks, velvets and other precious fabrics, haberdashery, toys, and domestic products such as spices and drugs that were weighed by 'the little balance' as distinct from 'the great beam' of the Grocers. By the time of the Company's first Charter of incorporation by Richard II in 1393, however, most of its members were merchants who dealt in bulk in all kinds of commodities except foodstuffs and precious metals, and their profits derived increasingly from trading abroad, particularly in wool and cloth. A group of Mercers engaged in export and import with the Low Countries via the port of Antwerp were chartered in 1248 as the Fraternity of St Thomas, and in 1564 (on a far broader geographical basis) as the Company of Merchant Adventurers. The latter contributed significantly to the development of England's foreign trade and sea power, and retained close connexions with the Mercers' Company and with the Order of St Thomas of Acon.

Much of the wealth accumulated by prosperous Mercers was devoted to charities and educational foundations—as, for example, the celebrated Sir Richard Whittington, three times Master of the Company, and four times Lord Mayor between 1397 and 1419. The romantic legend of his return to the City with his faithful cat lacks any historical foundation, but his fortune was certainly factual. During his lifetime and after his death it was expended and invested to establish schools and libraries, to rebuild Newgate and the Church of St Michael Paternoster Royal, to restore other churches, the Guildhall, and St Bartholomew's Hospital, and to endow the almshouse foundation known as Whittington College which still provides homes for twenty-eight old ladies.

Another eminent and philanthropic member of the Company was Dr John Colet, Dean of St Paul's Cathedral, who founded and endowed St Paul's School in 1510 and entrusted its

The Livery Hall which was opened in 1958

The Large Court Room

The Reception Area

*The **unique** private chapel of the Mercers' Company*

governance to the Mercers. When asked by Erasmus why he had thus placed his confidence in laymen rather than clergy he is reported to have replied that 'for his part, he found less corruption in such a body of citizens than in any other order or degree of mankind'. Sir Thomas Gresham, the founder of Gresham College, was another celebrated Mercer whose civic benefactions are still recalled. The first Royal Exchange, completed in 1568, was built at his sole expense, and he bequeathed it jointly to the City Corporation and the Mercers' Company.

In common with the other Great Livery Companies, however, the wealth of the Mercers rendered them vulnerable to enforced Royal loans which at times placed severe strain on their corporate resources. In 1573 the Company pleaded its 'decay' as grounds for exemption from contributing to a fund for the provision of wheat for the City's populace; but only fifteen years later, in 1588, its Master and Wardens were persuaded to advance a 'voluntary' loan to Queen Elizabeth I of the then very substantial sum of £4,000.

The Company was subjected to similar exactions on the part of Charles I, and subsequently by the Commonwealth Parliament; but its means were most seriously depleted by the Great Fire in 1666, which destroyed not only its Hall, Chapel and School but also incurred responsibility for rebuilding St Paul's School and of sharing with the Corporation the cost of replacing the Royal Exchange. In 1699 the Company's debts amounted to £60,000; by 1745 they had risen to £110,000, and repayments were unavoidably suspended. They were eventually settled, with some Parliamentary assistance, by 1804; and from then on the Company has been free to concentrate all its efforts on the promotion of its charitable and educational functions.

The Grocers'
Company

THE EXTANT RECORDS of the Grocers' Company date from 1345 with a list of the names of twenty-two men who formed a 'social benevolent and religious fraternity of the Company of Pepperers of Sopers Lane for love and unity to maintain and keep themselves together'. From other evidence, however, it is probable that this or a similar body had existed there for at least two centuries before this time, and may have superseded or absorbed the 'soapers' from whom the name of the thoroughfare derived.

In 1348 the Company was described as 'the Fraternity of St Anthony', and was evidently increasing in power and wealth. One of its ordinances promulgated in that year allowed widows of its deceased Freemen to continue their membership and to attend its dinners, although these privileges were forfeited if they re-married 'outside the brotherhood'. There is a gap in the records from 1357 to 1373, by which time there were 124 members, then described for the first time as 'the Company of Grossers'. The term derived from the French *en gros*, describing a wholesaler dealing in bulk, as distinct from a retail shopkeeper. It was apparently at first used by outsiders as a reproach, as instanced in a petition presented to Edward III in 1363 which claimed that 'merchants called Grossers engrossed all manner of vendible goods and those who have the merchandise raise the price suddenly by a covin (combination) called a fraternity and by counsel and assent keep the goods for sale till they are dearer'.

In 1386 the Company's ordinances claimed the right to check weights—certainly of its members, and possibly of other traders outside 'the mystery'; and in 1394 its Court acted in conjunction with some Italian merchants to petition the City Corporation in complaint against the unjust methods of 'garbling'—the cleansing or purifying of spices—then practised. The petition was granted, and one of the Company's nominees was appointed 'garbeller of spices and sotill ware'.

The first Charter of the Grocers' Company was granted by Henry VI in 1428; and in 1447 it received the exclusive privilege of 'garbling' throughout the Kingdom with the exception of the City of London. By this time its Wardens claimed authority to enter the shops or warehouses of all grocers, druggists and confectioners (later extended to include tobacconists) to check adulteration and to assay weights. The records include many instances of the exercise of these powers from 1456 on—among them the 'bags and remnantes of certayne evil and neynte pepper' ordered to be conveyed 'over sea' to be sold in 1561.

In 1348 the freemen of the Company were meeting in a hall close to the Church of St Anthony (hence, no doubt the name of the Fraternity at that time); but they later met at Bucklersbury, where they first became responsible for superintendence of the public weighing of merchandise, and introduced a regular tariff for the use of the public scales or 'King's Beam'. Richard II had granted the right to weigh wool to a member of the Company—John Churchman—who built a house for this purpose in 1373; and when Henry VIII allocated the Beam to the City the Company was entrusted with its control. These privileges continued until 1797, despite several disputes with the City authorities meanwhile; but the construction of the new Docks at Wapping finally deprived the Company of them.

The first Grocers' Hall was built on the site of the former house of the Fitzwalters in 1428; and from then and throughout the sixteenth and early seventeenth centuries the Company maintained its leadership in City affairs. In common with the other City companies, however, the Grocers were frequently 'requested' to provide loans for the King or Parliament. These loans were a very onerous burden and were met either by contributions from members or by mortgage

The oak staircase which commanded the entrance to the Grocers' Hall before it was totally destroyed by fire in 1965

The original Livery Hall was over 100 feet in length

The first drawing-room which was decorated by a frieze showing Charles II entering London after the Restoration

of the Company's property. The Great Fire of London in 1666 inflicted further losses from which the Company did not recover for nearly a century.

The Company's fifth Charter was granted by William and Mary in 1690 and its revised by-laws included ordinances against counterfeit wares, false beams and weights, and confirmed powers to garble spices. But there is no mention in the records of the Company of anything in relation to trade after the Great Fire and it is probable that monetary difficulties made it impossible for its control over trade to be maintained. Despite this loss of jurisdiction, its members fought to maintain its status and wealth, and today it still zealously discharges its many charitable commitments.

The fourth Hall which was built 1890–93 was unfortunately destroyed by fire in September 1965. The monochrome illustrations record the interior of that building, but the frontispiece of this volume shows the present Grocers' Hall.

The Drapers'
Company

THE DRAPERS' COMPANY, like most of the other Livery Companies, emerged from voluntary associations formed within the various trades for religious, social, benevolent and protective purposes. The term 'draper'—derived from the French *drapier*—originally applied to a maker of woollen cloth, and not, as subsequently, a retail dealer.

During the decades following the Norman Conquest most of the wool grown in England was exported to the Continent, where it was greatly prized for its superior quality and made into fine cloth that sold all over Europe—and some of it reimported into England. This trade was controlled by the Merchants of the Staple, and left the English economy at the mercy of foreign capital and dependent on foreign shipping, leading gradually to a decreasing number of weavers in this country. To correct this state of affairs Edward III prohibited the export of wool and encouraged the immigration of Flemish weavers to practise their craft and 'teach it to such of our people as shall be inclined to learn it'. This development of the home industry led to a need for the regulation of trade, and thus to the granting of the Company's first Charter in 1364. The increase of power of the Drapers' Company can be seen from that time, both within the drapery trade—from which tailoring and weaving were separated in 1385—and in the City of London. Such was its power by 1406 that a petition to Henry IV complained that the Statute of Liveries of Edward III was principally infringed by 'the multitude of the Company of the Livery of the Drapers'.

Blackwell Hall in Basinghall Street was purchased by the City in 1397 to be its sole market for the sale of woollen cloth. From 1405, in accordance with an Order of the Common Council, the Keeper of the Hall was appointed by the Drapers' Company, and the elections to this office are still recorded in the Company's minute books.

In 1607 the Company obtained a new Charter of Incorporation from King James I, in its ancient style of 'the Master and Wardens and Brethren and Sisters of the Guild or Fraternity of the Blessed Mary the Virgin of the Mystery of Drapers of the City of London'. The Company has continued to be governed under the terms of this Charter (apart from slight changes made by supplemental Charters) to the present day.

The trade in woollen cloth was officially regulated from a very early period and was frequently the subject of legislation. An edition of statutes in force in 1640 refers to fifty-seven relating to drapery; but, despite the monopoly granted to its members by Edward III, it does not appear that the Company possessed any statutory powers to interfere with the trade.

By the early part of the seventeenth century the Company's connexion with the trade had practically ceased—partly due to changes in the structure of wool trading, and partly because many members of the Company were no longer involved in drapery. Attempts were made to amend the latter situation in 1653 and in 1684, but without effect: the exercise of the Company's authority over its trade fell into disuse (although it has never been formally renounced).

Originally, the London drapers lived and traded in and about Cornhill, but during the late fourteenth and early fifteenth centuries they moved to Candlewick Street (Cannon Street). The first recorded Drapers' Hall, built sometime before 1405, was on the site of a house in St Swithin's Lane formerly owned by Henry FitzAlwyn, the first Mayor of London. The present Hall in Throgmorton Avenue occupies the site of the house of Thomas Cromwell, Chancellor to Henry VIII, purchased from the King in 1541 after Cromwell's execution for high treason and consequent forfeiture of property. The original house was rebuilt in 1672 after being destroyed

The charming garden of the Hall of the Drapers' Company

The Livery Hall of the Company of Drapers was built between 1866 and 1870

The Court Room where the governing body of the Company meets

in the Great Fire, partially rebuilt again after another fire in 1772, and almost completely rebuilt during the nineteenth century.

In the present day the Company maintains its traditional civic functions, but its major concern is the administration of its many charitable trusts, which include two schools, four sets of almshouses and a block of flats for old people, a number of pension funds, and substantial benefactions used for educational grants to needy students. In 1952 the Company established from its own resources the Drapers' Charitable Fund, from which grants amounting to approximately £200,000 are devoted to a great variety of charitable objects, including education, medicine and the arts at home and the provision of scholarships for school-leavers and university graduates to continue their studies in Commonwealth countries and the United States of America.

The Fishmongers' Company

THE ORIGINS OF the Fishmongers' Company have not been precisely traced, but it must surely have been one of the earliest of the ancient City guilds, as its trade pre-dates recorded history. The Romans are said to have imported oysters from England before their conquest, and throughout the middle ages all kinds of fish (both fresh and cured) formed an important part of the national diet, encouraged by the relative costliness of meat and the large number of fast days in the calendar. Salted haddock, mackerel and sturgeon are included in the scale of pontage duties of London Bridge in the reign of Edward I; herrings, fresh and pickled, were sent from Yarmouth and Hull, and lampreys from Gloucestershire; salmon were still netted from the Thames, and even whales caught off-shore were salted in preparation for the winter shortages. Among prices fixed by the King's decree were 3d. a dozen for sole, 1d. each for the best mackerel during Lent, and 2d. for twenty-five eels or a gallon of oysters.

There is reason to believe that a Charter was granted to the Fishmongers by Edward I in 1272, although they were among the guilds fined by Henry II for conducting their affairs without the Royal Licence. The first Charter limited the traders' profit to one penny in the shilling, prohibited the storage of fish in cellars, and buying before the King's appointed purveyors had made their selection. Until this time fishmongers were restricted to the vicinity of Old Fish Street, and fish could be landed in the City only at Queenhithe; but Edward I restored their right to trade elsewhere, and during the reign of Edward III they tended to concentrate around Billingsgate.

The first extant Charter was granted by Edward III in 1364, and confirms that 'the Mystery of Fishmongers had grants from the King's progenitors in ancient times'. In two further grants in the following year the King confirmed the Company's monopoly of fish sold in the City and gave it permission to elect four persons to oversee all dealings of the trade. Conversely, the Fishmongers donated £40 towards the Royal cost of the French War—only £1 less than the Mercers at that time—and another 10 marks in 1365. Their status and strength in the City was indicated by a list of members submitted to the Common Council in 1377, when the Company ranked fourth in precedence (as at present) and returned six members, the maximum number.

The question of precedence gave rise to a scandalous affray between the Fishmongers and the Skinners in 1341. Such quarrels were common enough at that time, and were usually settled by the Court of Aldermen; but in this instance the Lord Mayor intervened and condemned the leaders of both sides of the dispute to the gallows.

An Act of Parliament in 1380 declared the fish trade to be 'no true craft' and thus open to all, but it was later repealed and the Company's Charter was renewed by Henry VI and his successors, and that of James I is still the basis of its present powers. These entitle the Wardens to the authority of search over all persons 'selling, or having, possessing, or keeping to sell, any salted fish, salted herrings, fresh fish of the sea, salmon, stockfish, or any other fish whatsoever' to determine whether it is fit for human consumption. In this connexion the Company still appoints officials known as 'fishmeters' who examine all the fish brought into London, and its bacteriologist examines samples of all shellfish consignments, whether from home or abroad.

In other directions, too, the Fishmongers' Company retains closer connexions with the trade of its origin than most of the other surviving Livery Companies, and has statutory duties in addition to its Charter powers. It is directly concerned with the development of the country's salmon and freshwater fisheries and with the problems of river pollution, and helps to maintain the Marine Biological Laboratories at Plymouth.

The Drawing Room of Fishmongers' Hall, which contains the famous portrait of the Queen by Annigoni

The Livery Hall of the Fishmongers' Company

The magnificent site and exterior of Fishmongers' Hall, overlooking the Thames

Among the many charitable trusts in the care of the Fishmongers is that established in 1715 by Thomas Doggett, a celebrated Drury Lane comedian, in honour of the anniversary of George I's accession. On or about 1 August every year six young Thames watermen just out of their apprenticeship row from the Swan at London Bridge to the Swan at Chelsea in a race for Doggett's Coat and Badge—the latter engraved on silver—provided by funds bequeathed to the Company as trustees.

The Goldsmiths' Company

THE GOLDSMITHS ARE first mentioned in extant records in 1180, when they were listed among the 'adulterine' guilds fined for not having applied for the Royal Licence. They must by that time have been among the wealthiest of the City's traders, since their guild was fined the maximum of 45 marks. In the earliest surviving documents concerning the Guild there are entries relating to sums paid for religious and social purposes and for the relief of distressed members; only subsequently did it become concerned with the protection of its members' interests against fraudulent workers and tradesmen.

The Company's existence was recognized by Statute in 1300, when Edward I enacted the standards for gold and silver and decreed that no article made of these metals be permitted to leave the premises of its workman until it had been assayed by the Wardens of the craft and stamped with the leopard's head device. The first of the Company's Charters was granted by Edward III in 1327 and, besides giving its members power to elect their Wardens, specified that all dealings in gold and silver would take place in the 'High Street of Chepe' (Cheapside) or at the King's Exchange. The main reason for this regulation was to defeat thieves and to make sure that all gold and silver vessels offered for sale had been acquired legally. 'Whereas of late not only the merchants and strangers bring counterfeit sterling into the realm, and also many of the trade of goldsmiths keep shops in obscure turnings and by-lanes and streets, but do buy vessels of gold or silver secretly, without enquiring whether such vessel is stolen or lawfully come by, and immediately melting it down, do make it into plate and sell it to merchants travelling beyond seas, that it might be exported; and so they make false work of gold and silver, which they sell to those who have no skill in such things . . .'

Individual goldsmiths appear to have acted as bankers and pawnbrokers from an early period, accepting as pledges not only plate and jewellery but also items of value such as cloth-of-gold and fine table linen. Cheapside and its neighbouring streets were the principal locations of the shops of the trade, part of Cheapside being for long known as 'the Goldsmiths' Row'.

During the fifteenth century the London Goldsmiths were formally divided into 'native' (i.e. English) and 'foreign' categories, each of which was sub-divided into Freemen of the Company and 'Allowes', or licensed traders. Most, but not all, the Freemen were natives, who enjoyed the privileges of the Livery and were subject to the Company's control—as were the Allowes, but without its privileges.

The control of the trade under the Charters continued until the early eighteenth century, but the Company's powers were by then being questioned and difficulties were arising in their enforcement. It has been supposed that the problem may have arisen because the Charter powers derived from the Crown without parliamentary approval, and that the authority they gave to enter and search private premises and to inflict fines or confiscations were seen as an infringement of common rights of citizenship. In order to redress such grounds of objection the Company decided, in 1738, to submit a Parliamentary Bill, which became law in the following year. Although prepared by the Company's officials, and presented at its sole cost, this Act was accepted by Parliament as public legislation, and provides the basis of the regulations of the trade under which the Company's statutory authority is exercised to the present day.

The Act of 1739, still in force, repeats the terms of all the earlier Charter rights and regulations controlling the sale of gold and silver, and states in its preamble that 'The standards of the plate of this Kingdom are both for the honour and riches of the realm and so highly concern his Majesty's subjects that the same ought to be most carefully observed, and all deceits therein to

The staircase of Goldsmiths' Hall with the Company's banner and the statue of St Dunstan

The Livery Hall of the Company.

The Italianate front of the Goldsmiths' Hall in Foster Lane

be prevented as much as possible; but, notwithstanding the aforesaid several Acts of Parliament, and charters, great frauds are daily committed in the manufacturing of gold and silver wares for want of sufficient power effectually to prevent the same.' It is under this Act that the London Assay Office is regulated, and under the control of the Company, assays and hallmarks plate produced in this country and imported from abroad. Today there are three other Assay Offices, independent of the Goldsmiths' Company, at Birmingham, Sheffield and Edinburgh.

Another important function which the Company has performed since the reign of Edward I is called 'the Trial of the Pyx'. Its object is to provide an independent check that coins produced by the Royal Mint are of correct weight and of metal of the proper degree of fineness or formulation. At first the duty was performed at irregular intervals, but since the passage of the Coinage Act of 1870 it has been performed annually at Goldsmiths' Hall.

The Goldsmiths' Company retains much closer connexions with the craft of its origins than most of the surviving Livery Companies. In addition to its statutory obligations it has for many years promoted research, at Cambridge and elsewhere, into technical problems of the industry; and has encouraged high standards of design by means of liaison with trade organizations and sponsorship of college training scholarships and competitions for the design of important items of presentation plate.

The Skinners' Company

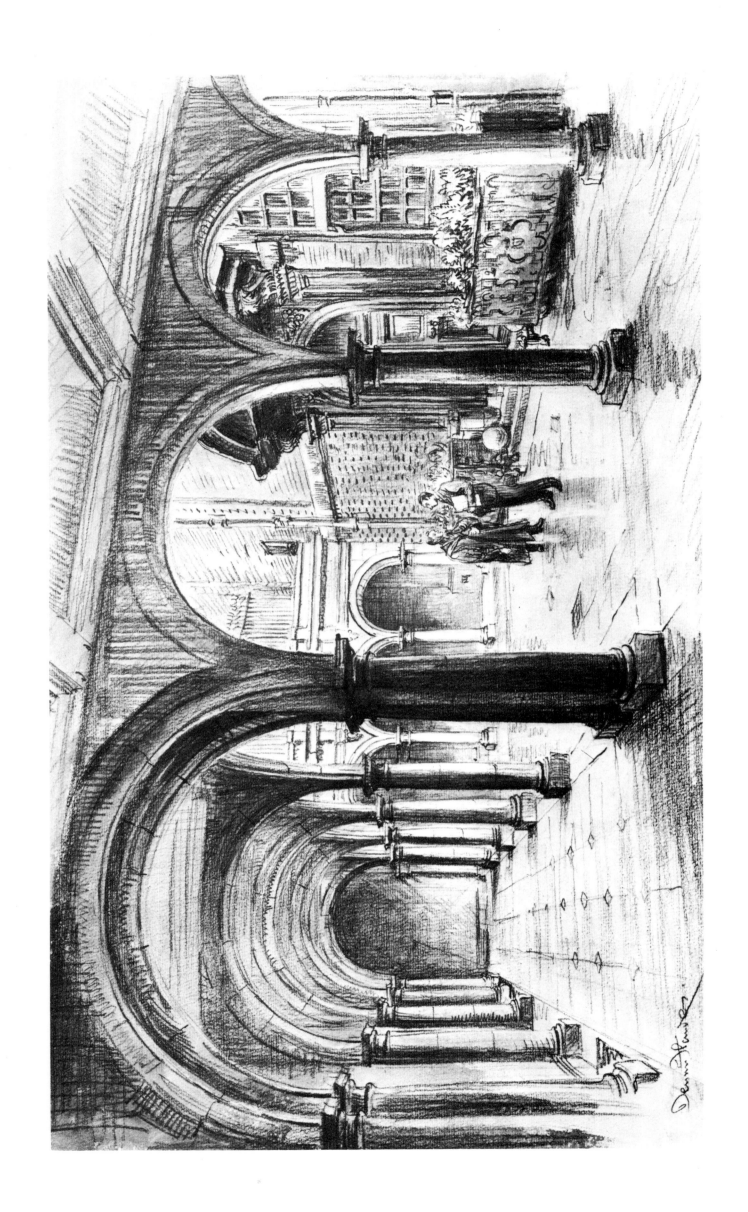

NO DOCUMENTARY EVIDENCE is known which indicates the origin of the Skinners' Company, but it is probable that the trade was well organized in the City before its first Charter was granted by Edward III in 1327. Stow related that the chartered fraternity was formed from two brotherhoods of Corpus Christi, at St Mary Spital and St Mary Bethlem respectively. It is more than possible that they represented the two quarters in which skinners then congregated: around St Mary Axe, and in the neighbourhood of Walbrook.

Edward III's Charter gave the Company effective powers to regulate the fur trade, and ordered that no skinner (or 'philippar') should sell 'old furs other than those taken from vestments, for as much as of the old furs and capuches as well the nobles as others of the community . . . believing them to be new, whereas they are old, are by the same philippars often deceived'.

These powers and privileges were confirmed by an Act of Richard II in 1392—'Having consideration of Our special Grace and for £60'. Even at this early date the Company was not confined to those working in the skinner's craft or trade. It had already absorbed the Tawyers' and Upholders' Guilds, and Richard II's Charter allowed it to admit 'any other persons whom the same they will receive'. A list of twenty members in 1445 identifies them as three gentlemen, a doctor, two butchers, one dyer, one joiner, one grocer, one silkwife, and nine of no named trade—but only one skinner.

The Feast of Corpus Christi was still celebrated by the Company until the Reformation with a procession 'through the principal streets of the City wherein was borne more than one hundred torches of wax costly garnished, burning bright, and above two hundred clerks and priests in surplices and copes, singing, after which were the Mayor and the Aldermen in scarlet, and then the Skinners in their best liveries'.

Extensions of the Charter powers were granted by Henry IV, Mary, and Elizabeth I, and it was during the latter's reign that troubles first arose between the Company's governing body and the working artisans of the trade. These arguments continued for many years and culminated, in 1605, in an application by the artisans for separate incorporation by letters patent, without either the consent or the knowledge of the Master and Wardens. A Charter of 1666 provided for the election of a proportion of working skinners to the governing body; but they were still refused recognition, and the Master and Wardens appealed to the Privy Council, by which the dispute was referred to the Lord Mayor to hear both sides of the case. The resultant report had the effect of confirming the terms of the Charter granted by Elizabeth I.

Subsequent Charters granted by Charles II, James II, and William and Mary confirmed to the Skinners the rights originally bestowed by Edward III. The Company continued to elect members from other trades, and a call to the Livery in 1738 lists a gentleman, a grocer, two linen drapers, an upholsterer, a glover, a tallow chandler, a butcher, a plasterer, a victualler, a rum merchant, a watchmaker, a feltmaker, a haberdasher, a wharfinger, a tailor, a timber merchant, and three of no description—but only six skinners. Nevertheless, the fur trade was still of importance, although no longer as flourishing as in former times, and the Company's intervention was sought on behalf of the artisans in distress. In 1733 a petition was presented to Parliament pleading relief from duties levied on coney skins; and in 1744 the proposal was made that the trade would recover if those engaged in it illegally could be prosecuted. By 1744, however, the artisans were again attempting to resolve their problems by means of greater representation at the governing level of the Company, and started a legal action with this object,

The cloistered courtyard of Skinners' Hall

The actual hall of the Company of Skinners dates from 1850

The Court Room is filled with pleasant fragrance of its cedar panelling, although it is 300 years old

which they lost. Similar proceedings were renewed in 1747, again with negative results; and the Company continues today to elect its officials according to the ancient procedure in practice long before the first Charter of Edward III. Among the curious survivals of this era is the custom of electing the Master by attempting to fit a cap on the heads of several members of the Court— and by strange coincidence it invariably fits only the First Warden.

Although the Company's functions as a trade guild have long ago become obsolete it still has many duties to discharge in connexion with its corporate trusts and properties. Among many foundations in its care is Tonbridge School, founded by one of its distinguished members, Sir Andrew Judd, who was Lord Mayor in 1550. The Company also maintains other schools, and almshouses.

The Merchant Taylors' Company

THE EARLIEST RECORDED reference to the Taylors as a separate craft occurs in *The Chronicle of the Mayors and Sheriffs of London*, which records their notorious dispute with the Goldsmiths in 1267 when some 500 armed men of each side came to blows one night and many of them were killed or injured. The brawl was brought to an end with the arrival of the Sheriff with the City *posse comitatus*, who arrested the ringleaders of both factions, thirteen of whom were executed.

The Taylors' earliest formal recognition was in 1299, when Edward I granted them the style of 'The Taylors and Linen Armourers of the Fraternity of St John the Baptist'. From references in the early records it is evident that its members were both tailors and cutters, in the modern sense, and also constructed the royal pavilions and military tents. 'Linen armoury' referred to the inner lining and padding of armour and the surcoats worn over it.

In 1326 Edward III honoured the Fraternity with its first Charter, which specified that no one was permitted to hold 'a shop of the mysteries' within the City unless 'free'—that is, admitted as a member of the Company. In 1354 the Taylors donated £20 to the Crown, which would place them in only the middle rank of the Livery Companies; but in 1377 they sent six members to the Common Council, thus equalling the largest then extant. In 1439, when Henry VI confirmed their Charter, they were granted the additional privilege of searching for, and correcting, abuses of the trade; and under this authority a search was made with the silver yard-stick at the annual St Bartholomew's Fair. Fuller powers were secured in 1502, when Henry VII re-incorporated them as the 'Merchant Taylors of St John the Baptist', with the monopoly of 'working, cutting or making of man's apparel' within the City and its suburbs and the right to admit 'whatsoever persons . . . they may be willing to receive . . . without the hindrance or disturbance . . . of any other art or mystery'. In addition to the right of search for defective craftsmanship or fraudulent measures, the Master and Wardens were then entitled to license every tailor and cutter in and around London, and to compel him to become a member of their Company if they approved of his competence, also to submit to the inspection of his work at any time.

In common with all the City Companies, the Merchant Taylors were often involved in disputes concerning precedence. In 1277 they ranked seventh, in 1403 eighth; but a little later they had risen to fifth place. Their major argument was with the Skinners, and in 1484 both Companies agreed to accept the ruling of the Lord Mayor and the Court of Aldermen. The decision was that they would take precedence in alternate years—unless the Lord Mayor Elect was from one of them, when his Company would take exceptional precedence. It was also decreed at the same time that the members of each Company must dine at the other's Hall twice in every year. The arrangement appears to have produced lasting harmony, and is still followed to this day.

The Company increased its wealth and power throughout the Tudor period, and by the reign of Elizabeth I was frequently under compulsion to provide funds to support the costs of wars abroad. Among other means of raising public funds were official lotteries, but when the Company was recommended to speculate in one of them in 1585 its Clerk recorded in his Minutes 'One byrde in the hande is worth two in the wood: if we get the great lot it will do us no good'.

Another reflection of the troubles of the period stems from the arrival in London of many refugees from religious persecution in France. Although in the long term they brought many benefits to the country, the government of the time had to institute a regular watch to protect

The Court Room

The New Hall, designed by Sir Albert Richardson, PPRA, was completed in 1959

The cloisters which contain the priceless hearse cloths, and relics which were discovered during rebuilding

them from mob violence. The Merchant Taylors, in common with other City Companies, were ordered to appoint 'Two discreet of their members' to attend daily at Aldgate to see that the Queen's order—'to use the French strangers well and quietly'—was carried out.

The Civil War provided further financial problems. In 1640 the Company was compelled to lend £5000 to the King, and the Lord Mayor ordered it to provide '40 barrels of powder and match and bullets answerable to that proportion' for the defence of the City. During succeeding years substantial loans were exacted by Parliament, requiring the Company to dispose of some of its properties. By the end of the Civil War the Treasury debt amounted to nearly £25,000— of which a tenth (all that was ever recovered) was repaid in 1668.

The Great Fire damaged (although it did not entirely destroy) the Company's Hall, and added to its financial burdens. As soon as the ruins were cool enough to be explored it is recorded that the Wardens retrieved no less than 200 lb of the Company's melted plate, which was sold for the benefit of the re-building fund.

The Merchant Taylors continued to oversee the measurements of cloth until 1854, but have since then relinquished their rights over the trade. They still maintain the many charitable trusts under their control, of which the best known is the Merchant Taylors' School, founded by the Company in 1561.

The Haberdashers'
Company

HABERDASHERS WERE ORIGINALLY a branch of the Mercers, also dealing in 'small wares', and the two were so closely associated that during the reign of Richard II certain Mercers were fined for entering themselves as Freemen of the Haberdashers. There were originally two branches of the trade, each represented by its own Guild, dedicated respectively to St Katherine and to St Nicholas. The former mainly comprised 'Hurrers' or 'Cappers'; the latter, dealers in ribbons and laces and similar goods, who were then known as 'Milaners' because much of their stock was imported from Italy, and from Milan in particular. The two Guilds were certainly in existence by 1372; St Katherine's was incorporated in 1448 as the Fraternity of St Katherine the Virgin of Haberdashers of the City of London, and in 1502 was amalgamated with the other and reincorporated as the Fraternity of St Katherine of Merchant Haberdashers by Henry VII. By a Charter of 1510, granted by Henry VIII, the title was changed to the Fraternity of St Katherine of the Art of Haberdashers in the City of London. By a Charter of 1578, granted by Elizabeth I, the title was changed to the Fraternity of the Art or Mystery of Haberdashers in the City of London, by which title the Haberdashers are known today.

Among the varied stock-in-trade of the haberdashery traders from the earliest times were pins, which in the sixteenth century were said to be imported to an annual value of some £60,000. Only a century later, however, when the Pinmakers received their Charter from James I, the English manufacturers are said to have rapidly 'exceeded every foreign competitor in the production of this diminutive though useful article of dress' and to have developed a flourishing export trade.

There were few haberdashery shops in the reign of Edward I—perhaps not more than a dozen in all London; but in 1580 every street from Westminster eastwards was crowded with them. They sold, amongst other things, 'French gloves, Flanders-dyed kersey, brooches and spurs from Italy, daggers and swords from Spain, Milanese caps, and tables, cards, balls, inkhorns, and silver buttons in great profusion'. Strype describes them as making 'such a show in passengers' eyes that they could not help gazing and buying these nickknacks'. A writer in the time of Elizabeth I 'marvels that no man taketh heed to it what number of trifles cometh hither from beyond the seas, that we might either clean spare, or else make them within our own realm; for the which we either pay inestimable treasure every year or else exchange substantial wares and necessaries for them, for which we might receive great treasure to the benefit of both public and private enterprise'.

Like all the others, this Company suffered severely during the reign of Charles I and under the Commonwealth, being forced to contribute to the many 'loans' raised from the Citizens of London and its Corporations. The Haberdashers are said to have lost upwards of £60,000 in this way by the year 1673, when an account was drawn-up with due reckoning of unpaid interest; and the consolidated debts were reputedly still entered in the Company's ledgers well into the nineteenth century.

The site of the Company's Hall was the bequest of William Baker, Citizen and Haberdasher, in 1478. The original Hall was destroyed in the Great Fire, and there is no description of it extant, but it was evidently large as it was used for the meetings of the Parliamentary Commissioners during the Commonwealth. It was rebuilt by Sir Christopher Wren, seriously damaged by fire again in 1840, and restored in 1864. The latter building was itself a victim of the Second World War and was replaced by the present Haberdashers' Hall in 1956.

A view of the Binding Room from the north end of the Livery Hall

The Livery Hall of the Haberdashers' Company

The Luncheon Room—the panelling of this charming room dates back to 1730

Most of the Company's early records were lost in the Great Fire, but its history has been relatively uneventful, apart from the prevailing troubles that from time to time have been common to all the Companies. In more recent times, the Haberdashers have concentrated on the management of their charitable trusts, which now number over one hundred, and include almshouses, grants to poor persons, educational grants and bursaries, and schools. Conspicuous among them is that of Robert Aske, who in 1688 bequeathed an endowment in trust to the Company for the support of a school for twenty boys. The original foundation was in Hoxton, but the resources of the trust have so increased under the Company's custody that it now supports two large schools. In all, the Company is concerned with the administration of eight schools, containing some 4,500 pupils.

The Salters’ Company

D.J. (after Shepherd)

SALT HAS BEEN produced in England from the earliest times: the Romans made pits and mines, and salt works spread throughout the kingdom are recorded in the Domesday Book. Salt was already a major commodity because it was used for the preservation of fish and meat, and it is in this sense, rather than that of the production of salt, that the Company derives its name.

One of the earliest references to the trade occurs in the household expenses of Edward I when, in enumerating the various expenses associated with providing fish for the royal table, the wages of the salters' man are mentioned. Salt fish was then a very common foodstuff eaten by people of all ranks. In 1302 Yarmouth furnished 100,000 herrings for the King's table, and in 1338 Edward III obtained 400,000 salt herrings for his army in Flanders. Thus, it is easy to see that the salters were able to become extremely powerful.

They existed as a fraternity from before 1349 but the first reference to them as an organised group occurs in 1394, in the reign of Richard II, when they were granted letters patent as the Guild of Brothers and Sisters of All Hallows, Bread Street. They are also mentioned as sending members to the Common Council in 1376. The Guild was undoubtedly first formed for religious and social, as well as mercantile purposes, but the latter gradually became their major interest.

Richard II also granted the Company a livery in 1394, when it was referred to as 'a Fraternity and Guild of the Body of our Lord Jesus Christ', which no doubt had supervision over some devotional works and sacred observances, although no details of them have survived. The Company was not formally incorporated until 1559, by Elizabeth I. This Charter gave the power to search the houses of London and suburban salters for bad merchandise and false weights and measures. James I confirmed this grant in 1607, and the right to own lands in 1619. During the Middle Ages the interpretation of the term 'salter' broadened and must be understood as including not only those involved in the application of a salt to the preservation of food but all those who dealt wholly or even partially in it—such as oilmen, drysalters and druggists—who, together with salt manufacturers and merchants and grocers (who made salt one of their trading commodities) have been and are largely represented by the Company's Freemen.

In 1455 Thomas Beamond, 'Citizen and Salter', bequeathed the land in Bread Street, on which the Salters' Hall had recently been erected, to the Wardens of the Company for ever, together with other property which would produce enough money to keep the Hall in repair. This Hall was situated conveniently close to the old market for fish, which was of prime importance to the Company's members.

The Company's Hall on this site survived until 1539, when it was badly damaged by fire. The replacement Hall was itself destroyed by fire in 1598. The Company moved to its third Hall, adjoining the Church of St Swithin, in 1641. This Hall, called Oxford Place, was purchased in that year and the Company remained there until the premises were destroyed by the Great Fire. Undaunted, the Salters rebuilt their Hall, but according to Herbert 'it was a small structure', as was to be expected since so much of their property had been destroyed by the same fire. This was the Salters' home until, after a century and a half, apparently dissatisfied with its size and dignity, they demolished it. The fifth Hall was erected on the same site soon after: a very striking and magnificent structure which survived until its destruction by enemy bombing in 1941. Due to post-war planning difficulties it has only recently been possible to select a new site on which to replace it, and it will be some time before the new Salters' Hall is ready for occupation.

The Hall of 1668 to 1824 from a drawing by T H Shepherd

The interior of the Livery Hall before destruction by bombing in 1941 (from photographs and old engravings)

Interior of Entrance Hall (drawn from old illustrations). The building was completely destroyed on the night of 10th May 1941 by fire bombs

Since their original trade has been superseded by the rise of refrigeration and other methods of preserving food, the Salters have turned their attention to these new methods and particularly their scientific background. In 1918 they founded the Salters' Institute of Industrial Chemistry, of which the main purpose has been the election of young chemists who show outstanding scientific and managerial abilities to fellowships and scholarships which allow them to pursue their studies. The Institute also provides funds for research in various universities and colleges, and has thus successfully adapted a medieval foundation to modern conditions.

The Ironmongers' Company

THE IRONMONGERS OF LONDON were the subject of official regulations as early as the reign of Edward I, although they were not referred to at that time as a guild. They were originally known as 'Feroners', and according to a record dated 1300 a complaint concerning them was in that year raised before the Court of Aldermen: 'For that the Smiths of the Weald and other Merchants bringing down irons of wheels for carts . . . much shorter than anciently was accustomed, to the great loss and scandal of the whole trade of Ironmongers'. As the result of this action three measuring rods of 'the just and anciently used length' were presented to the Chamber of Guildhall and to two overseers representing the trade who were empowered to seize any wheel irons found to be of improper length.

The earliest reference to a Guild of Ironmongers occurs in 1328, when the various trade and craft mysteries of the City made offerings to the King's fund for the costs of maintaining the French Wars. The Ironmongers contributed £6. 18s. 4d. and appeared in the eleventh place on the list. At this time they sent four of their members to represent them on the Common Council.

During the fourteenth century, and for long after, the trade appears to have combined both merchant and retailer functions: '. . . for, whilst they have large warehouses and yards whence they export and sell bar iron and iron rods, they have also shops wherein they display abundance of manufactured articles which they purchase of the workmen in town and country, and of which they afterwards become the general retailers'.

The Ironmongers became an important and flourishing community of the City, and several of them served as Lord Mayor, including notably Sir Richard Marlow (1410), and Sir John Hatherley (1442). Another indication of growing status was an armorial grant to their Guild in 1455. Eight years later, in 1463, it was promoted from a licensed fraternity into an incorporated Company by the grant of its first Charter by Edward IV to 'Our well-beloved and true liegemen—alle Freemen of the mistere or craft of the Iremongers of the Citie of London'.

In 1523 Henry VIII 'commanded to have all the money and plate belonging to any Hall or Craft in London', and in consequence of this exaction the Ironmongers' Clerk recorded that 'He had all our monies belonging to our Hall . . . and also we sold a parcel of plate'. In addition, individual Freemen of the Company lent the King sums ranging from £40 to 33s. Despite the slender hope that any of these borrowings would ever be repaid, however, the Ironmongers' sense of loyalty appears to have remained undiminished, since they expended nearly £12 on 'pageantry' in celebration of Anne Boleyn's procession from Greenwich to Westminster in 1533.

The Company's Charter was confirmed by Mary in 1558, and again in 1560 by Elizabeth I. The latter demanded from it a loan of £60 in 1575, and when told that the Company was not in a position to lend money at that time the Queen ordered its Master and Wardens to borrow it on her behalf on their own security. Indeed, throughout this period the Company's accounts show frequent payments—often of considerable amounts—to provide men and arms for the service of the Realm. The problem became even worse during the following century, although the Ironmongers made all possible efforts to avoid involvement in the Civil War. Unlike all the other Companies they resolutely refused to contribute their share of the £50,000 loan demanded from the City by Charles I in 1640—although later in the same year they did subscribe to a 'voluntary' Royal Fund. In 1642 the Company again refused to pay its assessed quota—but this demand was from Parliament, and the following year it was renewed in the sum of £1,700 towards the defence of the City against the Royalist forces. The Master and Wardens protested that they were unable to contribute at all, due to numerous previous exactions never repaid;

The beautifully panelled entrance hall of the Ironmongers' Hall

Ironmongers' Hall was opened in 1925

The Reception Landing with its statue of Beckford and the Gainsborough portrait of Admiral Hood

but despite all efforts of evasion they were compelled to sell all the Company's plate in order to satisfy the Commissioners.

The trade was originally concentrated around Ironmonger Lane, between Cheapside and Gresham Street; but during the middle years of the fifteenth century the Ironmongers migrated to Fenchurch Street, and in 1457 a house there was acquired by the Company and became its first Hall. This was repaired in 1540, and rebuilt in 1587 because it was by then 'ruinous and in great decay'. Although not damaged by the Great Fire, it was in considerable danger, and for several nights the Company's Clerk employed men to keep watch and to be prepared to remove its valuables and documents to safety. A new Hall was rebuilt on the same site in 1748, but its foundations proved unstable and it required frequent repairs and alterations. This was the only one of the City Company Halls to be damaged by an enemy bomb during the First World War, after which the site was abandoned and the present Ironmongers' Hall was built in Aldersgate in 1925.

The Vintners' Company

THE TRAFFIC IN WINES with Bordeaux and the neighbouring provinces is said to have started in 1164 through the marriage of Henry II and Eleanor of Aquitaine. The Normans were the great carriers and their vessels must have been regular callers at Botolph Wharf near Billingsgate, which Edward I granted to the Vintners. The rental for the wharf was a silver penny yearly, but the King also profited by exacting a duty of two tuns of wine out of every cargo.

The Vintners themselves were divided into two classes, the Vinetarii and the Tabernarii. The former were importers of wines and included the great merchants who lived in the Vintry near to the wine wharves. The latter were the keepers of the taverns, inns and 'cork-shops' over whom the Vinetarii exercised constant control. They were recognized as a Company during the reign of Edward III, since in 1365 they contributed £23. 6s. 8d. to the French wars and in 1377 they sent six members to the Common Council.

It is from this period, also, that their first Charter dates, for in 1364 Edward III granted the 'mistery of Vintners' the sole right to buy wine abroad and retail it in England. It also enjoined that foreigners should be entitled to sell their wine wholesale only to the Vintners. They were also to see that all manner of wines should be sold at reasonable prices in taverns, and were given control over the taverners.

In the Middle Ages there were very stringent regulations for tavern-keepers—for example, they had to close as soon as the curfew sounded (under the pain of a penalty of half a mark) and they had to allow customers to see the wine drawn from the wood (to prevent them selling lees, or the droppings from the taps, or good wine mixed with dregs). In 1364 one John Penrose was found guilty of selling 'unwholesome wine . . . to the deceit of the common people, the contempt of the King, to the shameful disgrace of the officers of the City, and to the grievous damage of the community'. His punishment was made to fit the crime—he was imprisoned for a year and a day, forced to drink a quantity of the 'unwholesome liquor', had the remainder poured over his head and was expelled from the fraternity of Vintners for ever.

Stow records that in 1427 the Lombards were found to be 'corrupting their sweete wines' and when this knowledge was transmitted to the Lord Mayor he ordered that the 'heedes of the buts and other vessels in open streetes be broken, to the number of fifty, so that the liquor running forth, passed through the cittie like a streame of raine water, in the sight of all the people, from whence ther issued a most loathsome savour.'

Another duty devolving on the Vintners was to oversee and regulate the measures used in their trade. Foreigners could sell only by the tun, the pipe or the hogshead, and these measures, as well as the smaller ones used by the taverners, were frequently found to be defective. Another measure of control came from their ability to license tavern-keepers. Before a new tavern could be opened the prospective taverner had to apply to the Company, and the Wardens and others would view the proposed premises to see whether the site was suitable. They were very rigorous in applying these criteria and, in 1629, when Nicholas Banaster wanted to start a tavern in his house the committee of inspection found it was 'near certain alleys, in a back place which lends itself to secret wickedness, debauchery and drunkenness'. Also it had a bowling alley and a pair of archery butts where poor people 'will spend their thrift and cause brawls'. The licence was refused.

Edward VI created some problems for the Company when in 1553 it was enacted that 'the number of tavern keepers in London should be limited to forty; in York to eight; and in other

The elaborate staircase of the Hall of the Vintners' Company

One of the finest seventeenth-century interiors in London—the Livery Hall of the Vintners' Company

The Court Room of the Vintners' Hall

cities and towns in proportion'. This would have greatly injured their trade and they were quick to petition Mary to be relieved of this burden for 'if it suddenly should be put into execution, we should be constrained to put away our apprentices, journeymen and other servants, and break up our households to their utter undoing'. Having been confirmed in their old rights and privileges by Mary these were re-confirmed by Elizabeth in 1567; but, in 1577, the Queen signed a statute which allowed a larger number of people to keep one tavern (Freemen of the Company of Vintners could not keep more than one). The result of this was such an increase in the number of taverns that the Vintners petitioned the Queen that 'great multitudes do daily set up taverns, not only such as neither are nor ought to be allowed by the said licence, but also foreigners and strangers, and in excessive numbers, and in places inconvenient, and without being charged to the keeping of good ordinances, to the great hurt of the commonweal . . .' This petition was granted, and James I granted new Charters to the Company in 1603–4, 1611–12, and 1614.

The Great Fire destroyed its Hall and the Company had to resort to inns for their meetings until it was rebuilt in 1671. As time has passed the Company has had to reorientate its connexion with the wine trade but this connexion has never been broken and in the twentieth century is probably stronger than it has been since the middle ages. The Company is closely concerned with wine trade education; it offers scholarships and bursaries and, in conjunction with the Wine and Spirit Association, has founded the Master of Wine Examination. Those who are successful in this gain the highest qualification in the trade. The Hall is in constant use for wine trade lectures and meetings.

One of the Company's many interesting links with the past is the right of its Freemen to sell wine by the glass without a licence in London and within 'three miles from its walls and gates' and in certain other cities and sea ports, and towns on the London-Dover and London-Berwick roads. Another surviving privilege, shared with the Dyers' Company, is the right to own swans on the Thames. Records for the expense of 'upping the swans' go back to 1509 and a member of the Court of Assistants is still appointed each year as Swan Warden. It is his duty, together with the herdsman and swan markers and those of the Crown and the Dyers' Company, to make an expedition once a year to mark the cygnets with the Company's swan mark. The other, more formal, links with the past consist of the charities with which the Company has been entrusted and which it still administers.

The Clothworkers' Company

Dunster Court, off Mincing Lane, the site of the Hall of the Clothworkers

THE CLOTHWORKERS, in common with all the other trades concerned with the manufacture and conversion of cloth, appear to have derived from the ancient Guild of Weavers, of which an extant Charter granted by Henry II refers to 'liberties and customs in the time of Henry my grandfather'—thus, it must have been in existence in the early twelfth century, and may indeed have been of pre-Conquest origin. Under the terms of this Charter the Guild was entitled to regulate the trade of clothworkers, drapers, tailors, and all the various crafts that related to clothing; but it eventually became so powerful as to threaten to rival the City's civic authority. This led to its suppression by King John, and the various trades that had formed the original combination became separate guilds.

Among those that emerged from this disintegration were the Fullers and the Shearmen. The former were congregated around Whitechapel Church, which is still called St Mary Matfellon, after the herb then known as 'matfellon' (fuller's teasel) which grew nearby and was extensively used in the craft. The Fullers were formally incorporated by Edward IV in 1480. The Shearmen, who turned the cloth and levelled the nap, were referred to in 1456 when certain 'Citizens and Sheremen of London' acquired 'a tenement and mansion house lying in Minchin Lane for the use of themselves and their heirs for ever'. From a patent roll of 1479 it appears that, although not then incorporated, the Wardens of the Fellowship had power of search over their own craft 'according to the laudable custom of the City'; but in the same document the Drapers and Tailors were assured that no charter would be accorded to the Shearmen. They made repeated efforts to this effect, however, and were eventually successful in 1508, when they received their first Charter from Henry VII.

Twenty years later the two trades were united and reincorporated by Henry VIII as 'The Guild or Fraternity of the Assumption of the Blessed Virgin Mary of Clothworkers of the City of London'. This Charter provided the usual privileges of a distinctive livery, of holding land and other property, the election of the Master and Wardens, the right of search and the punishment of offenders, and the prohibition of foreigners from plying the trade unless they became members of the Company on such terms as were imposed on them. It is notable that its livery was granted to the 'brethren and sistern' of the trade, so that women presumably enjoyed equal membership rights.

Prior to the amalgamation there had been a great deal of contention between the Shearmen and the Dyers as to the relative rank and precedence of their respective Companies. The conflict was finally resolved in 1515, when Sir William Boteler was Lord Mayor: an Order of the Court of Aldermen in that year recorded that the Wardens of both mysteries have 'lovingly and obediently' agreed that 'the Sheeremen shall go, stand and ryde in all processions and other goyings . . . next before the seyd Wardeyns and ffelisshippe of Dyers . . . without any further strife of debate'. Thus it was that in succeeding to the precedence of the Shearmen the Clothworkers' Company became the last of the twelve great Livery Companies, and the Dyers became the first of the minor Companies.

During its early history the membership of the Clothworkers' Company comprised mainly persons engaged in the trade, but by granting its freedom 'by way of composition and redemption' and by the admission of Freemen's sons who were not themselves of the trade it gradually relinquished its exclusive character. Of the five individuals named as Master and Wardens in the Charter of Elizabeth I in 1560, for example, all but one were of other occupations. However, the Company's Court of Assistants was recruited from 'the most judicious and skilled artisans,

The Livery Hall of the Clothworkers' Company, which was opened in 1958

III

The reception area, just off the Livery Hall

whose livelihood depends upon the manufacture of cloth'. In those days Clothworkers were defined as 'persons able to wet out or damp the cloth in the stocks, then put it over the perch and rough it sufficiently with card or teasel, then set it, and afterwards shear it by hand or frame with the broad shears, and to finish the cloth by planing or pressing it'. The Company continued to regulate the trade by searching and confiscating or fining for bad workmanship until as late as 1754, when it was recognized that this exercise of its prerogative would no longer tend to 'the better skill of the art or mystery of clothworkers, or for the common profit and commodity of the Company'.

Since that time the Company has concentrated on its many and varied charitable functions. It administers over one hundred trusts, many of them concerned with the welfare of the blind. Its contributions to education are also substantial: in particular, the Clothworkers' Departments of the University of Leeds, the City and Guilds of London Institute and the Mary Datchelor Girls' School at Camberwell, of which Foundation the Company is the Governing Body.